EVERWHEN

AKRON SERIES IN POETRY

AKRON SERIES IN POETRY
Mary Biddinger, Editor

Titles published since 2015.
For a complete listing of titles published in the series,
go to www.uakron.edu/uapress/poetry

EVERWHEN

Anne Barngrover

 The University of Akron Press
Akron, Ohio

ISBN: 978-1-62922-244-8 (paper)
ISBN: 978-1-62922-245-5 (ePDF)
ISBN: 978-1-62922-246-2 (ePub)

A catalog record for this title is available from the Library of Congress.

∞ The paper used in this publication meets the minimum requirements of ANSI/NISO Z39.48–1992 (Permanence of Paper).

Cover image: Hibiscus and Plumeria, copyright © 2022 by Manuela Koosch, papertopetal.etsy.com. Cover design by Amy Freels.

The book's epigraphs are excerpts from:
Anna Lowenhaupt Tsing, *The Mushroom at the End of the World: On the Possibility of Life in Capitalist Ruins*, Princeton University Press 2021.
Emily Wilson, *The Odyssey*, W. W. Norton & Company, 2018.

Everwhen was designed and typeset in Utopia by Amy Freels and printed on sixty-pound natural and bound by Baker & Taylor Publisher Services of Ashland, Ohio.

Produced in conjunction with the University of Akron Affordable Learning Initiative. More information is available at www.uakron.edu/affordablelearning/

For Vedran

I'll always walk with you, even until the end of the world.

Making worlds is not limited to humans.

∞

—Anna Lowenhaupt Tsing,
The Mushroom at the End of the World:
On the Possibility of Life in Capitalist Ruins

Now goddess, child of Zeus,
tell the old story for our modern times.
Find the beginning.

∞

—*The Odyssey,*
translated by Emily Wilson,
Book I (l. 9–11)

Contents

I Begin in Scrolls

This is an old story. Once in a time
long past I unfurled my little page.

No one knew I could move. Light
hushed in wind and shadow. I wrote

the book of ocean tides, the book
of ancient moon. Time was time.

In the morning hour, I searched
for the sun to cast a spell when it

was still of help to wish for a thing.
There was and there was not. I made

the sound of paper. A seed travels
through time and books are made

from leaves. I was painted as water
was being strewn and sand was being

poured. Art is based on plant life.
Bran here, flour there. Faithful

representation, though, is rarely
the point of form. Return my story.

Feed me bread and water. I folded
up in darkness. A bell rang in time

and I opened to the world. Red,
redder, this tale is over. This book

comes to an end, but the story yet
remains. Scrolls have relentless power.

I've told you what is coming.

Persona Poem

I am a mind-body problem I am this era's golden age I play a certain role in folklore I am a plant-based dye I'd like to think I'm economic I taste a sugared rind I am a willow beauty I am a red vase vine I am indigo and saffron I am a beneficial weed I am history

through artwork I am an egg protein
proof that yeast will rise I am a
controversial prize I am a person
your future archive I am studied
I mean is *to smoke through* I am
note and heart note too I was born as
dead duck I am the broad dark
memories For luck I hang from
keyholes I am a lavender puppet
perfume My body a satchel I
ruined field Nights I become
I become an owl to hide
chastised for mocking
wolf who can take off
newly collected
into theory I am
scholars I am
I am structural

I am the bread the broken pieces I am
subarctic island I am the most
cut from a textile outline I am
as a postmodern conjecture What
rectified as a spirit I am the head
a sprig of myrtle I appear as a white
blotches you see deleting long-term
windows For luck I'm rubbed on
When I pray it's to give up my
am a walking onion I am the
a hare to steal butter Nights
from rage I become a lizard
sorrow I become a she-
all her skin I am the
tales I am translated
a favorite among
their focal plane
coloration I am

a fragrance wheel I am in love with idleness I am an orchestra of wind I am a gelling agent I harness the strength of knots I am the inscrutable ocean I am underwater sheaves I am forever in middling blue I am the reader (you) I am the writer (me) I'll never be at peace

Ceres in the Uncreation

I tried to write a warning
                  in chaste trees and pumpkin vines:
the worst men of our lives will return
          to us in more ways than one.

Preordained, how women must watch
                  this reincarnation of cursed stone,
the curdled constellations
          of anger and loneliness you men rewrite

and call myths of heroes. Call yourselves heroes.
                  Don't you ever learn? I am the goddess
of law and order. I am the goddess of food
          plants and cereal grain. Without agriculture

your precious bank note civilization
                  collapses into slag. Your precious
small farms. You treat them how you treat your women:
          admonished husks, aberrant gourds.

I am the guardian of women and girls
                  in their times of transition,
the points when they're most vulnerable. Which means
          at all times, which means I cannot protect them.

My name translates: *to grow*. Did you know
                  I was chained? From him I birthed
another daughter along with the child
          of a horse. You want to say, I did this to myself.

If I had not lived
                  in this body. If I had not run. Was it a son?
Even the goddess of vessels becomes a vessel.
          The summers you created broil your crops

and your cities. You'll fight long wars over water
                    that evaporates into smoke.
Perhaps you have forgotten? Your stars were never
            undying. The Fates are women, also.

"A Lot of Stuff Happened, and I Quit Being Normal"

—Meme from the anime Boogiepop and Others

No one can reach me when my hormones spike. I go off
to live in a forest of bird's-nest ferns. People are aggressive
that I am not special. What I'm feeling is a condition
of being human. I guess everyone thinks they're dying
all the time and daydreams about getting in front of death
so they don't have to worry about it anymore. Cool!
She has endured a series of catastrophic events. If someone
complains that a book made them depressed, I'll read it.
When I have a day off, my mind decides to pretend
I'm itching and burning just so it has something to do.
My endocrinologist says I'm sensitive. My dentist says
I'm sensitive. My gynecologist says I'm sensitive.
My allergist says I'm sensitive. My therapist says I'm so
sensitive, she has to reorganize our healing schedule.
When I get acupuncture, the needles keep popping
out of my earlobes. That's supposed to mean anxiety.
An essay someone else wrote about my ex went viral,
but people assumed I'd been dramatic for seven years.
Why is my bird's-nest fern dying now? I kind of enjoyed
the MRI. Like a rollercoaster through a cave, snuggled
in tight like a boxed cigar. They were looking at the center
of my brain, seed mushed inside a pumpkin's wet head.
Excess cells have a great time sloughing off hormones
to convince me that I'm dying. Literal symptom: *sensation
of impending doom.* Fear *backed and packed* like fish irises
in that Elizabeth Bishop poem. I feel safe when I hear
a really accurate description. How can people be left
and just continue living? Reading my tarot cards,
I keep turning up stars and swords. Reading my coffee
dregs, all I can see is water. *Where are you going after this?*
The medication shadows my vision for about four
to five minutes after lying down. I chill on the couch
and wait for it to return. Sometimes, all I can see
is a black orb in front of my eyes. *That goes away
for most patients over time.* Last summer, I wanted to feel

bad enough so people would believe me. I spilled coffee
on my laptop and lost a thirteen-page essay. I know
I'm going to receive a lecture, but I don't trust whatever's
in the Cloud. I wrote my essay back from memory
on printer paper in the mall Starbucks before my turn
at the Apple store. I wrote enfolded by glass sunlight
and giant ferns. Sometimes, there's no one who can see
anything real about me. I wrote it back word for word.

Tennessee is Burning

Two kids wanted to set the South on fire.
That's all we know for now. Its flames so bright blind men could see,
the wildfire ravaged the mountainside, felling telephone wires

and trees fuzzy with rain and copper leaves. Prior
to late November, a drought languished for three
months. One match kicked, and now the South is on fire.

I am nowhere near the mountains, but I can smell the air
lit thick with particulate and charred debris.
The light today burns weak, the sky looks smeared, and *fire*

has so many meanings—noun, verb—the entire
island of Manhattan could fit inside the wreckage of Tennessee—
and no one cares that the South is now on fire

because if we shout *fire!* we could mean *liar, liar.*
We could mean to ring all the bells at once, a prophecy
said of volcanoes, a vivid light, a splendor. There is green fire

and there is red fire, and through the South course rivers of fire,
a false or misleading beacon no one could have foreseen
except that we should have. The South has always been on fire.
It just keeps reeling me back in—it's a luminous body, a star.

Heather Lives in Missouri and I Live in Florida But Our Friend is Very Sick in California and We Want to Light a Candle

—for N. K.

By the time we arrive to the churches, they're locked
for both of us, and my sky's cramped with thunderheads.
My dress clings like a sweaty fog, and a thousand miles
westward Heather's baby squalls. On my way home
a train spasms its jagged leg past gas stations, liquor stores,
and houses that squat August-damp as mouths,
those holy sanctuaries of geckos and winged
roaches, whose foundations brace for hurricanes
and sinkholes though they were never built to honor
revelation, and my God, tonight I am a hypocrite.
To pray with a match is to ask for stillness, but all I want
is motion. When Heather gave birth in Missouri
and I was in Ohio, I stared into the sunset so hard I felt it
break around me the way you finally exhale
once you realize your breath has been shallow for hours,
and if you really think about it, a candle moves so fast.
Wax leaks from the wick's center then rebuilds
itself into something new, and in my neighborhood
palms shed their skirt flakes and rusted fronds
into the road like parts of a human body that startle me
though there is nothing of the body about them.
I see lungs everywhere now. The sum of our three
ages doesn't amount to a century, and all I have to offer
is the rain. Lord, I am earthbound to this storm.

The Crying Bird

From the parking lot I hear it scream.
      Near midnight, the body

of water by my apartment
      is a swamp hemmed into pond,
         dark that deepens

another dark, a jaguar's black
rosette that shimmers upon black fur.

      No beak, no wings, no sound

         of flight or leaving

when it's easier to hear than see.
I'm the scientist

         I've always wanted

      to be, timing each wail
      for the velvet comfort

         of taxonomy, the need

to agree on what it's called.

         Limpkin.

What happens when the name
      for a thing is all wrong? Secrets

bloat the wetland—hidden grotto
      behind golf course
         tavern, empty

Gatorade notched like a sconce
into cabbage palm. But things fit

    into place so easily. Where I live,

        there must be apple

snails and moon
snails, too, water

        lettuce and a way to build

    nests from rushes, to wait
    out the night on floating plants

        and not care who hears this knell.

Whippoorwill of tropic hour,

            crippled

bird, lamenting bird—
    when you keen

the river halts its rise,
    and I don't know what
        I believe anymore.

Who writes our new story,
bird in dark water that no one can find?

    Remember me. Remember me.

    Only its cry knows where it's gone.

Ceres in the Red Tide

The ocean retches and collects. We have mistaken you, our water
    god, for a savior of fallow pastures, your ruling

    planet for a fixed star. A message blinks through the ether:
Let's work on improving this together. But it's too late

for prayers when salt animals distend heavy
    as sodden paperbacks, toxic script penned on every folio.

    They cannot hide in their septic shells,
and you cannot return the light

energy you harnessed from the sun. Don't you remember? I tried to run
    from you with hooves and quick-reacting

    tendons—I transformed myself into a mare.
Neptune, brother, you would not rest until you overpowered

everything that needed blue to breathe.
    You plunged your own house into the Great Dark.

    You sealed our throats with rocks. Haven't you always
proved the impossible equation, never seen

with the naked eye, discovered only through ancient math?
    I could not escape from you by horse

    or will or sheath of grain. The ocean remembers.
The planets remember. My body remembers everything you've done.

My Hair Falls Out

and I could write a list
                    of all the places I find it—

                              my hair a dark signature
my hair splinters of glass

            I pay someone

to soften in light—
                  but I don't think I want to anymore.

    Not on these nights
                        I get so deep in thought
                                                I tip
                  backwards inside my head

        like a mushroom
                        caving in on itself after hard rain.

Not when a barred owl flies straight

at my car like it knows me and my hands
                              knock back from the wheel

              as I watch it suspended
                                    in the tornadic glow
of headlamps, great wings
                        pumping as it rises
                                    talons ripping

          at the swamp-curdled air. Tell me again

how a woman's hair
                  will loosen its hold

after she opens herself

to the world

and a newborn's will, too.

My mother says when she'd lift me

from the cradle I'd leave behind

tiny black feathers on the blankets

before the hair of my new body grew.

Haven't I always been drawn

to what clings

before the fall?

No one tells you it's not becoming   to be strong.

I am always writing

a list of places

of where I've been

and where I'm going.   I always leave

so much behind.

And if you could crack open my chest

pick apart what goes wrong

why nothing ever stays for long

and why things break   so easily

what would you find

because I've paid good money

I want the answers—

What can you see

besides all that madness

(*I feel it, I know it's there*)

I mean, besides all my missing hair?

Owls Come to Us

when they are lost and we break/open their pellets and draw them maps/
out of lizard tails and jawbones/delicate as bracelet clasps/when the forest
is lonely/when the palms no longer speak/when they are really mourning
doves/when they are stuffed and amber-eyed/when they are monuments
to desperate stones/when they are stenciled topaz and gold/when we peel
plastic from our irises/when our cyber activity falls through/when we gift
them in twos/snug together like mug and spoon/when they follow us
silent as watches/as prophets/as harbingers/as witches/as banners of war/
when night falters/when night fails/when we expect an emergency/but not
the emergency that happens/when time stops for us/when we live
in glass jars/when we try to run away/when we run through the hours/
but the clocks stay the same/when we are omniscient/when we are limited/
when we develop a strong point of view/when we want to save you
and you and you and me/when the maps become circles/when the maps
go away/when we want to send a message/though there's nothing left to say

Why I Couldn't Write

Because I took everything out
        of my drawers
                and piled it on the floor.
Because it was rush hour at twilight in Central Time.

                Because poems became like marbles—
there was no way inside
                and I had splintered myself already.
                                Who cared
if words fizzled and rhymed? Who cared if the lines broke
                      like powder
            from a stale donut in my mouth
                and I had to hold out my hand to catch them?

Because I wore a lead apron.
            Because they saw me dancing alone
      in a lilac dress and thought, *how sad.*
          Because I would stare at the ceiling
                    and there was nothing.
Because I would stare at the television
      and there was nothing.
Because I would stare at the walls and there was nothing

          except telephone wires curled into cobwebs.
Because I couldn't get a job.
            Because I drove through Missouri
                    I drove through Illinois
                    I drove through Indiana
                    I drove through Ohio
                    I drove through Kentucky
                    I drove through Tennessee
      and exit ramps didn't matter.

Because I wanted to be a block.
            I wanted to be a paperback, slid
                into a bookshelf, safe and contained.

I came across ski boats of many colors. They stood
        upright in a half-circle like ancient ruins.
                                  Whatever.
    The image no longer stuck in my mind like a penny
                and nothing rendered anymore.

Darkness poured over everything
      as though the sky were a tipped jar of molasses.

There was no thinking my way out of an X-ray.

                I added the chemicals back into my brain
      one by one, row by row—
Gumdrops lined the roof of a house made of crackers and candy.
        My brain of swirls and loops.
            My brain of sacred decay.

Because the veins brightened
                    in my eyes.
        Because the people who loved me cried
            and I couldn't—not in years—
I don't know why.
                   (That's a lie.)
Because I'm not supposed to talk about what happened,
          and if I were doing yoga,
    then what was the problem, anyhow?
        Yoga gave me heat rash. Yoga gave me ringworm,
                pink spirals on my thigh.
        I didn't talk to anyone
although I went there to make friends.
        I learned that I was stronger,
(quieter)
    than any man.

          Because I went through every object in my house.
      I drove old towels to the animal shelter,
then I put everything back in my drawers.

It was cleaner, less cluttered,
only filled with what I needed

but not at all the same.

Pelvic Ultrasound

—Ovaries: from Latin: ovarium, *literally* egg

I've waited to see you for years now
but when you light up the black screen

like night-shining clouds, I become
nervous and turn to the side. In static,

sound waves form you as sand does
to shipwrecked glass. How is it

that you and I always manage to live
among radicals—spiders electric

with poison, cat who sashays indoors
after a burglary, dirt clod that morphs

into a cricket frog? A gecko scurries pink
as sticky tack along the bathroom wall.

How it twirls to an embryo in my palm.
It's expensive to get a good look

at you, though you're not mine
to interpret what's wrong. If anything

it's a hypnotic display or a book
we hurled in the road. Once we broke

a bush with a loaf of bread, thrown.
Once we broke a bush with a car's hood.

The next day its bumper was smeared
with indigo. Any woman knows how

many colors can present themselves
in blood. Something must've happened

to make you go rogue. We used to connect
fragments of ice crystals. We needed chaos

and carnivores. Even wolves can change
the way a river runs, so what have we done

to cast biology into anarchy and fade
from our distinctive glow? Oh, you shells

along my vertebrae and the vertebrae
of my mother, you have hidden from me

an ocean's depth, you of lunar odes
and filament, gossamer and tendril.

I can't see much in the dark,
but I've felt your whispered pull.

We all are in need of rewilding.
You don't have to do this alone.

Ceres in the Mass Extinction

I'd like to say we would've fought a war

                         if that had happened here, but the truth

is we, too, wove lies with our looms

           and called it breaking   news. Those random apostrophes in

           grammar—

Everything is possessive.   Everything belongs to someone else

                       but no one wants to pay.

The answer to *how could you?*   will never come so I learned to stop asking.

                Some people want to suck

out their own contagion and cast it onto corpse

                flowers, wild rice, and the star-shaped heads

of Georgia Aster—a bridesmaid blue

                that perfumes shaded edges and rights-of-way—

onto dark-eyed porpoises   shy deer with solitary horns

        redfish and rockfish   the one they consider *a good friend.*

It doesn't make sense   and now I feel a particular kind of pain:

            You hurt me

to prove how consuming yours became.

How does it help me to say you love me still?

Earth folds over herself like punched and fermented dough.

Look at your pain now.

Gone are the fluorescent amphibians.   Gone is the Large White butterfly

its wings a lucent invitation you won't ever receive.

Gone are the muscular cats from your wall art

and the rasped sonata in high fields.

Gone are the coral reefs, hot colors blinking out   each death a porch light

we won't drink under any more.   Even sand disappears

the way I do as you draw

what you need from me then flick off your brain:

not here enough to be the same   not gone enough for you to care.

I Always Wanted to Save the Rainforest

but now I live in a rainforest

and the thing I can't save
is me. Let's get to that later on.

A rainforest should be studied
in fours: emergent layer, canopy,

understory, forest floor. Self-watering.
Oldest ecosystem. My doctor explains

that the brain speaks to gland hormones
which speak to the ovaries

which speak to the uterus—or something
along those lines. I try to write

it down as fast as my hand can move.
An osprey flies above me with a fish

caught in its talons. The fish still looks
me in the eye. What is it they say

about a bird of prey overhead?
I'm afraid to google my fortune.

I know I sound paranoid, but the rainforest
is a cutthroat environment.

One must innovate
in order to survive. They tell me

nine vials of blood is less
than it seems, but if my bad

numbers are from stress, I plan
        to sue Paul Ryan for damages.

Just don't write about
        climate change! The word

cervix is polarizing, and no one wants
        to hear about your pelvic floor,

complex though it may be.
        What is it they say about women

and our bodies? Sometimes we feel
        an unconscious reflex to guard

ourselves against a world hell-
        bent on taking everything away.

And sometimes when I sleep
        I wake up to teeth

that no longer fit in my jaw
        or hips that ache from aggressive

curling into a creature of the soil.
        The forest floor is the most intricate

layer of the four. Light can't reach
        me forever. What is it they say

about *sympathetic overload*? I have
        my students write a research paper

in which there's a solution
        for every problem. I ask them why

did I structure the assignment
        this way, and they don't know

enough about despair to answer.
     I could list all those who poison

and seize, but the rainforest works
     to rebalance the numbers. My God.

Do women and rainforests
     have to do everything?

I don't live in a real rainforest.
     It's just a forest that's humid,

dark, and tropical, so dense
     I could find my way inside

and you might never see me return.

The Dread

A new love it's like a new baby you can't believe it'll last

I shouldn't say what I fear nor should I write it down

so I chant into the silence between

lightning and rainless thunder maybe if I memorize the parts of a bell

yoke and crown my head bewildered on shoulders weak

as a bridge a waist after the echo from a sound ring

how the locket of my phone holds a scrap of your hair

still it can't find you your lips or your mouth something bad

hovering in weak angles tree petals I can't name pink or white or gray

in a certain light a boy playing a game across the street where

he yells *I can't think* *of anymore colors* but there you are suddenly

my heart's storm it has passed all jade and aquamarine

when a tongue strikes the inside of a bell that's the sound that breaks

sometimes but always moves when it does it makes the bell ring

The Prayer Plant Speaks

I don't hate myself. I'm just self-aware and open
a little too early for evening vespers. Who couldn't use
more faith in any form? Sunset glares the same golden
light as a salt lamp clicked on. Your tomes refuse
to become embers. By nightfall, I ache but rarely bloom.
New World tropics don't do it for everyone unless
you're unburdened by diurnal rhythms or heirlooms
of clandestine purple. Gaze upon my glowing dress,
ever spooled and spiraled. Trail my creeping rootstock
back to where I first learned the definition of *grace*
and how it always seemed like blackmail. I can't talk
about unmerited favor without my leaves bracing
for close. How holy am I, to move without wind?
I am action, I am verb: I unfurl, I rise, I bless and sin.

Elegy for Fallen Palms

—after Hurricane Irma

I learn the facts about what we've lost:

palm trees don't form annual rings.

You'd find their age in the Bible or Quran, old as oil
    palm, fan palm, or windmill palm:

I learn these descendants of a common line.

Assyrians believed the sign of eternal life

was a palm beside a stream, but what if the men
    who poison rivers are always the last to drink?

Yellowed fronds mean too much rain.

It's hard to start over after a great change,

but if they're not cut for tables or sold as seeds,
    palms can outlive a home. And I'm so tired

of Midwesterners in boat shoes

who tweet, *Why would anyone live there?*

from their Puritanical woods that expire
    in annual gray. Because people who reside

in paradise deserve to suffer sometimes—

oh, but they'll vacation here! *It's unnatural for you to live*

where you're supposed to unwind. Queen palm,
    wild date palm, sugar palm or wine:

I learn the five hands of palmistry.

My hand is a wood hand, its knuckles thick

and fingers long, my mind stubborn and heart
        often wrong. What scares me most is the idea

            of *deep time*, or *everywhen*—which is a breath

        away from *evergreen*—though not at all the same.

The Earth remembers our sins, for time is not
        a tree trunk pushing forward but the wheel

            within that churns and scars,

        like how when I was thirteen the junior high

librarian stopped me in the hallway and insisted,
        But your family was in the basement once the tornado hit

            your house, and I had to shake my head, *no.*

        How teens drove to my neighborhood, parked

next to the Red Cross. They wanted to see roots
        gutted from soil, brick chimney that smashed a car.

            They brought popcorn for themselves.

        And I'm not easy to move to tears, but still I cried

for the maples and oaks that fell in my backyard.
        What I mean is, trees take the wind

            to spare the walls. Bottle palm, spindle palm—

        in a garden on Mauritius there grows

the loneliest palm, single specimen
        of a single species, most solitary of any kingdom.

It's enclosed in a box of metal wire,

a dot on a dot on a map of the world that's strewn

with broken palms. I learn flowers once glowed
on this last palm in the colors of white

and cream. Humans tried to intervene.

It hasn't bloomed in years.

Aubade with Myself Leaving Myself Behind

We parted at dawn in the Christmas tree palms.
        The older fronds had already started to die

from lethal bronzing. Baskets of red berries
        spilled into the swamp. Insomnia, a rumor

of wild hogs rooting in humid fog. Dawn
        and her fingers tipped rosy with spoonbills.

We read the inevitable graffiti slashed under concrete
        bridges. It advised us to condemn

several businesses and philosophies. Some gods.
        Some plants recognize the evening

by folding their leaves like hands in prayer.
        As children, we sorted buttons into families.

We wouldn't rest until all of them were named.
        Their houses were books that stood upright

as cathedrals that required a forest of trees
        to build them. A forest for every page. A page

for every daughter, never for sons. No sons.
        We ate our last cheeseburger, shot through

with a syringe of bourbon. The bite broke
        the glistening corners of our mouths.

Outside our doctor's office, roseate spoonbills
        took flight. Tests showed blood

in our urine and an imagined fire in our mind,
        real numbers too low and real numbers

too high. Only birds brighten as they mature.
           All night we wondered if maybe the trees

had run out of love for us. We dreamed
           that a palm frond grew legs and chased us

through the overgrowth. Our vascular system
           glowed in the dark. Maybe love had run out

the way a light bulb sometimes flickers
           then explodes. Glass shards, involuntary

seashells. The gulf, a morose bathtub. We parted
           in nouns and verbs, splitting time

like the hour in a painting versus the hour in a living
           room during a hurricane no one plotted

until the unlatched windows blew. Dawn became
           dawn became dawn became dawn

even though it stormed. I couldn't know
           the one when everything would change.

I Serve My God Pineapple Upside-Down Cake

because he demands hothouse eyes and delayed
manifestation. He requests my best side
hidden then flipped upright, wetly visible
only for his decree. Look at the golden ring
and cherry topping, retro and crystalized
as living room stained glass. I serve my god
clementine cake made from ground
almonds and six eggs. It's easy to lie
about how many oranges I can go through.
It's a cake of pulp and rind, a stepping stone
to the potential he knows I can reach
if I just concentrate on what he wants from me.
I serve my god lemon poppy seed cake,
zesting over a bowl until my shoulder aches.
Three times the glaze pools on the yellow flower
plate. Three times the base falls apart.
But the taste—so tart, so sweet. I suck my cuticles
and plead. I serve my god a carrot cake.
It's clogged with nuts and raisins, and I can't
move after grating roots with a rusted tool.
He is most displeased. The icing, too thick
or will not thicken. Layers collapsing like a cave.
I serve my god his birthday cake. I research
all night long. Its buttermilk, well shaken.
The batter's air bubbles slapped away. Its flour
comes from a red box with a picture of a swan.
His favorite icing, chocolate sour cream. My god
wants and wants from me. I make it perfectly
but still he doesn't believe me when I tell him
that pineapple comes from the ground
despite how I point to the row of blue-green spikes
growing in acidic soil. He wants me to show
him what I mean, to get down low. Maybe then
I can prove to him what it is he already knows.
He says, *I always had faith you could do it.* He says, *welcome.*

The Lamp Inside

In my past I lived upon a hill
                                present as a jar
            of light and snow, the woods empty

as ideas—impossibly, the ochre soybean fields
            fenced in white, owned
                        by a CEO whose barn housed

            a zebra, off-brand, striped the color
of coffee. I was young and in love
                        with my own doomed sense

that I couldn't belong anywhere
                        or with anyone. Early winter
evenings at my dormitory window,

            I brooded in the liturgical
blue over the inherent tragedy
                        that I'd never transcend the walls

            of this body. Spellbound,
I followed the sacred geometry
            within snowflakes kissing the glass pane.

                        Worlds and worlds
            glimmered below in the houses
                        down the hill. The woods parted

so I could see the lamp inside every room,
            families moving through hallways surely
                                    as rivers. No one

            bed-struck by panic. No one alone
                        in the terror of syntax—
            it is possible and also very likely, it is possible but very

unlikely, it is impossible, for it is in the unreal past—
	that haunted my future, years away. Still,
			I must have known it had marked me.

				Maybe *twilight* and *winter*
	are synonyms the same way a pocket watch
			and a clock tower both keep time.

And I *am an I*, falling off. Forevermore, light
	unfurls darkness, snow warms the bare trees.
			I see only what I want to see.

Ceres in the Field of Bones

Be real with me   for once   and answer: So one season
      of destruction   is not enough for you?   I'm not sorry

I was never drawn to you like I was drawn to the high sea.

Somewhere along the way, I developed an internal ocean.
      Underwater, there's still agriculture. I can swim

deeper than darkness goes. When you took my love
from me, I could not bear to look at flowers anymore.

Accounts vary. Stories unstitch to make me smaller

but I remember what I wanted:
      to slash at the root, to rend my nails

bloody in the dirt until I found you—
How do you kill an undead god? Raze the barren

strawberry, coltsfoot, wine cup, the cut-and-come-again.
In the trees   magnolia petals perch like swan

napkins, cream. They brown sweetly as banana peels.
      Tear them in fistfuls from their branches.

I can't stand you seeing colors
when all I see is wind   and brine tide pools. No starfish. Nothing

to point at that's mine. If you must spare the poppy,
orange-sick and lustful   then break a record of spring rainfall—

      a super bloom we can view from space.
May the fields glow like daughters
      before you poison them all.

The Hibiscus Talked to Me

—after Chavali Bangaramma

She had questions that required
deep and political thinking. *Surprised*?

she asked and I was
ashamed though generous

with the water I gave, wanting
her life force to exalt and fulfill me,

believing that to be her role.
I wanted her unfussed

by annihilation. I wanted her blousy
and loud, shattered

with singularity, lit as if by electricity.
She lived by the rule of three:

more color, more fragrance, more
size. But I was afraid to look

her in the eye. Large and seeping
color, it was a mouth possessed

by lipstick, a hypnotizing maw.
Out of it sprung a strange, long column,

an erotic yellow thing. She made me
flawed and fevered. I wanted to decide.

A big plant is like a big planet,
her petals red-veined and windswept,

creamy velvet, chiffon. If she must speak,
the world preferred her muted.

We don't take ones like her seriously—
tropical yet short-lived,

showy because she knows
what her heart is, centered and swirling.

She'll fade in the evening shadows,
sleep through the darkest winter of our lives.

The Fear

This serves as a list of everything I can't eat when it takes me

wet fries in pastel pink sauce segments of gold

fish basket we share standing sour cherry dumplings

a gift you brought me carried a long way you hide behind your back

chocolate and cream the outer planets revolve telling us something

in their movements it doesn't sound good but shrimp glazed in mayonnaise

that was what you ordered I miss it the bread sags cheese spat like gum

a cookie I can't finish a crepe fed apricot jam did you know everything

is what I want I'm a glass cabinet which was built as locked rooms

when one door shuts a window shuts too one summer I scrubbed dirt

from a bouquet of carrots it still tasted like minerals the only protected thing

I ate in months a decade ago nothing can prepare you for the rot

the unspooling embryo return to your putrid hovel of a life gone bad

egg in the bowl swear to me my mouth will open again one day promise I will eat

Flamingo Casino Lobby, Four A.M.

When I open up like this,
        I stop eating. Our pizza smells
                like fuchsia. Around us, smoke travels

hallways, wraiths unraveling
        their scarves. Earlier tonight, people napped
        and cried beside
                an aquarium where fish wear

faces painted as dolls. *That must have been terrifying…*
        We say this
        to each other till the words blur
with our spending money.   *The past, the past…*

there is no such thing.
                        Not when our terrifying lives
thrash around inside us,

        bubble in our throats, beat
their fists against walls of skin.
                  Money passes

through many hands. So is joy the distraction
            from death or is death the distraction
        from joy? And if I am just

            a distraction to you …

                    if, if…

I can't see through the window, but I know
        flamingoes must be sleeping
                in satin darkness, lined up like cocktail

shrimp poised on martini glasses.
        Their necks twist back like bread dough,
                        knees bandaged in guava-pink gauze.

        But I know who I am.

I am well aware
        of what it's like to look
                imagined. I have never been able to hide.

Though what is faith this late at night
        but dots of oil on my mushrooms, oil
        on your pepperoni? I just want

our terrifying lives
                to mean something
before the sun comes up. Maybe this is all

I need to say to you: I can hold on
                        to any story, even yours,
even my own. It is almost dawn,

and I'm still hungry.
                We only have a few hours left to go.

I Tell My Sister I Learned Space is Like a Donut

—for M. A. H.

in that it wraps around itself and never ends

but the kicker is that it also never *began*, or rather, *begins*

because time is like that, too—

a donut or bagel or Danish, and so is God. *No, no!*

she shouts and pushes back from her chair.

She muffles her ears. *I can't take it! Infinity freaks me out.*

I remember when I, too, was that afraid,

ever since I saw Cookie Monster devour the moon.

Now, I find comfort in what I cannot explain.

Or perhaps *comfort* is not the word I'm looking for.

These days, I hold infinity at bay like sugar

caramelized in my teeth, the seeds and stones muscled

in my shoulder blades, my gray-eyed children

of whom I dream—smaller than punctuation

and cradled in the place where our bones go

unnamed. The Greeks stared and shook their heads

because the pelvis was unlike anything

they'd ever seen, formed of three bones that fuse

together once we've grown. For women,

it happens when we bleed. Mine took forever.

The doctor squinted at my hipbones glowing

in their X-rays like slabs of cod encased in ice on display.

Underdeveloped was the word he penned

for me at fourteen, my body all right

degree angles in a one-piece bathing suit,

my spine nonlinear, my hamstrings tight as cello strings.

Still, I cannot be contained. On the darkest night

of this future year, the air is too dry to light the solstice

lamps we planned to set sail. And I scan the darkness

tonight as I never have before because I have lost

someone, and she isn't coming back.

I wish I had taken Calculus. I wish I could interpret

the numbers and graphs, the geometry of a spine

that bends until it halts—a medical miracle, unforeseen—

the difference between *actual infinity* and *potential*.

I wonder if this is where we go when we die—

the innominate place the Greeks knew

but couldn't say—where we begin again in another world,

another plane. The ancients had so many names.

I wish I could ask them how long it will take

her to catch up to where we are now,

and what if, when she finally arrives, we look away?

The last word my friend wrote me was *deserve*.

How I'd love to share a donut with her in a café.

Ceres in the Burning Rainforest

darkness now falls   as little else does

the roof a potent symbol   fires are not   wildfires not

old-   growth trees could change

promised to weaken and open

a political problem   misplaced colonial mindset

if degraded beyond   a complex story

to fill in the gaps   common myths sell us   beef and soy products

dry out the forest   an island   the island a trap

smoke its own   forest its own   mountains of smoke

sealed inside   a shopping mall   no safety in fruit stands

                            planet of smoke   your crops won't grow

                            we don't have the full picture yet

                            we could be looking at thousands of tiny fires

people have lit them   without fear

the first real sign   repeated   for how long

this isn't the full story   all those animals and microbes

this could be the worst moment   all that desire   the people

the soil   when wood is burned and does not have much

sense of identity or belonging   the rainforest can't become a story

breathing isn't a metaphor once it's gone   it won't come back

                            once it's gone it won't come back

do you hear me   what did I tell you   I won't come back anymore

When I Lie Awake in Pain at Night, I Think about Creation

like how it can only bring more suffering, as before

newness springs from nothing, which bears no expectation
      so therefore doesn't feel. Black-winged bird, inkhorn

of my brainstem—you shielded your egg for an island's age.
      It broke into the world. The story goes: our bodies guard

us from what hurts. I prefer etiology, a study that disengages
      with ideas of time and space, than a planet doused in mud

or insect spirits alighting that first cave. When I fainted
      in the blood lab, I tried to push away the chorus of three

women who chanted my name as if from very far, saints
      of ammonia towing me from a dark sea. I didn't want to leave.

Perhaps that's why *I'm sorry!* rushed through me in a gasp—
      I was nothing, I felt nothing, I was free from pain at last.

The Cats of Imerovigli

slink like shadows of owl wings
        along walls cool and curved
as seashells pressed to quiet earlobes,
        wear faces more angular than feline
            as if they were born in a thicket
to mothers who vanished in cliffside's maw,
        prowl the limewater caverns,
            blue-domed churches, and roofs
glamorous with sun where Instagram models
        preen in gowns that flap like thunder's hair,
        though they'll never reign
as these yellow-eyed goddesses of wind, as the bells
        that summon our memory of prayer,
            orange syrup cake, grilled tentacle
pink as conch's flared lip where the tide rushes
        in, as the ghosts of sailors, floral bruise
        of fog-grown tomatoes,
as the cats who slip through the pearl corridors
        of their city lit like music at nightfall,
        who do not beg beneath tables
or outside the sloped, azure doors but wait
        for low hands that glitter with fish scales,
        their moon a caldera of milk.

Praise to Our Basement Airbnb

Praise to the well-drained soil and stone-cast
walls, Victorian-style house painted the careless
color of egg cream and slotted as a beehive,
house we only entered through the side door
like a secret we could finally share. Praise
to the iron-wrought gate, to its double lock
and key, and the dark gloss of concrete steps
leading down. Sweet pull-out sofa, never slept on.
Sweet teal curtain separating our rooms, tender
as a moth wing, never drawn. Praise to the kitchen
made a kitchen by sudden tiles, half-empty tower
of hazelnut Keurig pods. Only soup spoons.
Only skim in a lofted fridge. Praise to the voices
of residents doing their laundry next door
and to the soft mechanic click and whirl. Praise
to the Blue Star donuts we didn't discover till
the last morning, their chocolate cardamom glaze,
dough-fried tang of orange powder and olive oil.
And oh, how there'll be never enough praise
for the bed in that basement—our first bed,
that did not belong to either of us, with its star-
patched blanket and gingham sheets, upon
which daylight's slant from the hopper window
cast our waking bodies as if we were characters
in a play written long ago. Praise to the camellia
by our door bursting in tropic joy, its marbled
fuchsia blooms wide as outstretched hands.
Praise to this whole city of cool-season rain
flowers, to the sun and moon swaddled in fog,
the once-volcanic mountain above the river
and the mossy forest beyond. And praise even
to our basement bathroom with its two-in-one
shampoo thick as mayonnaise and its porcelain
ring, slick as an ice rink, how I fell in the shower
and cried out, *I'm ok!* before I hit the tub's lip.

Praise to your shocked face and eyes bright
with worry, how you did not hesitate to reach
down and pull me back up into your arms,
to the way you held me, wet skin pressed tight
against skin, as though we'd stay here forever,
as though you couldn't imagine letting me go.

The Night My Number Tripled

in my recent bloodwork chart, I saw it and I fled.
Panic ripped through me like sallow gas

and as an animal would,
I must have believed
I could hide from my own leaking math. Pregnancy

or tumor—those were the options
and I wasn't sure which one I wanted
less. Around and around I went

in my apartment parking lot as if pursued
through carmine alleyways. Oh, my blood
and its mutable omens. My brain and its end

of days. It didn't matter
that the dusk was beautiful in the early
rainy season when the sky takes

on the plush and tropical hues of stone
fruits so I could remember that I lived
in a place far but not too far

from the ocean. Magnolia flowers sat
primly as teacups. Gray and white
birds shone where they flew like lights

off moving water. It started to get dark.
My parents couldn't find me.
My boyfriend was asleep

halfway across the world. I walked as if to leave
behind my body, though I understood
I had to receive what it offered me.

So this is what it means
            to be alone, I said inside myself
        and to myself as a violet wind pushed through

the palm fronds above me, initiating a sound I recognized
            like the rustle of dry grasses
        before a storm, as the first

stars opened their eyes to nightfall
            the way an apocalypse can mean
        to reveal.

Ceres in the Global Heat Wave

Have you ever tried to sleep
            as winds thrash a lofted room

            the way a god of evil flogs
a wooden ship at sea? You feel

very small. If it weren't
            for cliff gusts and morning

            fog, we'd perish like snails
do on this dark and dry land.

They've been trying to live
            since the era when islands

            weren't yet islands but a part
of seedlings' collective dream,

white and spiral. I am not
            from any country or generation.

            This doesn't take place anywhere
in particular, except for now

maps look like they're screaming. Too hot
            for ruins. Too hot for roads.

            Fake popcorn flowers
on real cobs. Butter's gloss undermines

the ruse, as if we required hyperbole
            to prove what went wrong.

            I'm rubbing the apocalypse
in your face, I guess, since I don't get

to be moody otherwise. If men are mad
        at me, they hurt me or they leave

        with the blue stoneware
of my heart, and I never uncover it again.

Tonight, I'm the hottest I've ever been.
        I figure if that star

        doesn't move by the next time
I look up at the sky, it must be real.

Art needs an artist, words need a writer,
        and stars need to be believed,

        but what can I say about faith
when I've given the last of my warnings?

        I loved you in the marginal
seas and those not defined

by currents. I loved you with salt
        on my lips and in small sounds

        too numerous to list aloud.
I've been trying to live

since the era of your silence, which fills
        with trapped air like a gasp

        that goes on and on, and I'll never
be emotionally detached enough for you

to take me seriously. I can't save
        every slug on ash and asphalt,

        but I'll touch their damp bodies
with hands not clean enough to hold.

Too hot tonight for rain. Too hot for eyes
to close. I lie awake all night

listening as you take the world
from me—little by little, then all at once.

So This is What It Means to Be Alone

I said to the prayer I rub into my fingers To the scalloped and sun-blanched roofs I said to the dark bowl filled with apples and avocadoes To the old face in a new wall To the fleeting and the common To the scars along my jaw To history and prehistory To multiple vowels in a row To any transitional phrases I said to every brightly colored door To my pinched nerve and my anemia To the opened boxes of purple spice and orange clove To the fish market with wet floors and octopi shaped as stars To the sweat I wake up to in the crook of my legs To the smoked mussel pasta and cheap yellow wine To the hero's journey I never believed in To my solitude that has always been an illusion To the wind preparing ruins To the solar salt and sea brine I said to the mural with a dog as a mouth and a pillar as an ear To the kittens small as cupcakes on dirty ancient tile To my child selves and future selves though I can't imagine going on I said to the machine beating in my father's heart and the Cycladic blue of my mother's eyes To my sister and friends and cousins To the green bottled beer at the secret beach bar To the clothes wires stretched in alleys and the rush I get from leaning over To the Museum of Broken Relationships To luminescent vibrations To the trapped gas in my digestive system To the shaking of my thighs To the donkey wearing a rug with silver bells To the cooked and baked cheeses To the one that tastes like apple pie To the bougainvillea unrelenting To my confusion when I misread To the soft parts of a dead animal To the house it leaves behind I said to the ocean that knows everything but won't tell me what it finds

The Air Plants

You don't see us as our own
                creators, but you are not
the only artist here. Our root system
                was designed to anchor.
We don't dig—we cling
                to your telephone wires,
tree branches, bare rocks, wherever
                conditions permit us to draw
from dew and atmosphere.
                Art is about choosing to stay.

We make an impact where we land
                in our light seeds and silky
parachutes. We mean and do no harm.
                Look for us in the rain—
dusted with a little silver, rosettes
                sipping water. You can't live
on air alone. We may build
                a fragile architecture
but as we grow we curl into ringlets.
                We drape as strands of hair.

We may flower once
                in our lifetimes. We may not
flower till the end of our lives.
                Our blooms arrive
as midnight or as a purple quill.
                We flower when we know
we're getting what we need.
                Our name means *upon a plant*.
We are both part and whole.
                You are limited by your
imagination. You are not the only
                one with a dream.

Künstlerroman

In the beginning, I kept waiting for you
to leave. Here's the rising action: I'm just pointing
out a pattern along my journey. Once, I was left
over swirly bagels, left over making his bed.
A friend walked out during happy hour
and I never saw her again. Now I can't bear
the smell of grapefruit and gin. My family split
over gluten. Ever since, people keep trying
to take what is sweetest from me, what I want
most to have. Left over a yoga bag. Left over
a bundt cake I burned then taste-tested with my hand.
For the party, the hole was covered by a strawberry.
I am choosing to write in the passive voice
because there is nothing left after leaving. That's a lie.
They're always coming back, and there's this place
two inches below my belly button where
if you press down, it brings release. It's a rope
being yanked, a knot in necklaces and string. I cramp
at the sound of so many names. If you follow someone
but refuse to speak, that's called *orbiting*. I keep
getting served these articles online. There's this place
in my neck like a tiara of seedlings. I want you
to grab me there and never let go. Writing is hard
on my nerves and on my bones. Why did they raze
that blue trailer to the ground? And why did they set
fire to the no-longer-walls and no-longer-doors?
Because there's always something new and living
by the side of the road: sandhill cranes and their chicks,
the color of custard and soft as calico; three guitars
for sale, painted and propped against a pickup.
But who would throw a perfectly fine cooking pot
onto the shoulder? Years ago, I burned my wrist
stirring chili after he said my only job was to help him
get into heaven. I told the therapist he made me see
if I wanted to stay together, *I'm not sure if I can trust*

my own reality anymore. Shouldn't that have been a sign?
This was the shrink who referred to women as *brides*.
We are arriving at the part where I'm supposed to
either find some acceptance or turn away in arrogance.
And wasn't I already scorned for doing both?
My art has always worked like this: I make it
for you and I give it away. It hurts and you leave.
It hurts and you leave. We've reached the end now.
We're back at the beginning. You're still here.

I Proofread My Friend's Last Essay

she never finished before she died, and I connect

my old phone to its charger for the first time
        since a week after she'd gone. It doesn't work.

I mean it does, it still turns on—
        our messages preserved from beyond

eighteen months ago now, pinned
        honeybees crystalized in their own

sugar and gold, in what they have made
        and taken and made and given, together—

but this isn't what I need.
        I need to talk to her. I need to ask,

how did you write your sentences the same
        way a river flows, each pause a deliberate

water stone? I need another kind
        of punctuation mark to reach out and hold

on to like an anchor, like a hand,
        but I'll always have this larger question

about time. I forgot this morning we push
        the light forward, the clocks bewildering

me in their senseless moving on. I'm not ready
        for this draft to be final one.

I need to find a new way to talk about the love
        and pain I have felt every hour

since our parting, the love and pain
        that have bloomed around me

like the trumpet trees in their gusts
        of blush and lilac and sun-drawn

yellow, the color I've come to associate with her
        whenever I see it. Wild and clever,

how these trees show their fullest selves
        in the depths of midwinter, when all

seems dark and we've been so long apart
        from our final letters, but I've read

that trees can talk to each other underground
        in their roots and in their cells, far deeper

than first thought. She has changed
        me a season's measure—some people

are born again and again, find each other
        as different versions of the same question,

or find each other in the question, and know.
        I press my palm to the laptop, the phone

screen, to the crushed yellow flower that falls
        open like a song, to the heartbeat

of her words she's ended on. My pulse is a text
        message—I'll keep trying to hit *Send.*

To the Solstice Moon Over Red Rock Canyon

How can you be the same moon I knew
in Missouri, flushed by prairie fires, a marble

flicked down my gravel drive; as the sea-
worn Florida moon who eavesdropped

above the island Blue Parrot Café, anemic
face spiked with palm fronds; as the moon

smudged by fog over the hills in Tennessee,
the center of a tongue yellowed as though

from whiskey sours; same as the Ohio
moon who first taught me to say its name?

Each night, carried to the patio, I'd startle
or I wouldn't—you come and go, require

my earliest wreck of faith. Barely late
afternoon, shadows measure the canyon

in lavender. Winter means little to a desert
still you rise like an arm-swung lantern,

bright as a knot of snow. Was it only half
a year ago you couldn't find me sleepless

and sweaty, my heart flitting a rented room?
Restless, I crossed the street one evening

to celebrate the anniversary of a lakeside bar
I hadn't visited before. Hippies and I danced

in the sand to a twelve-piece brass band
that erupted from the back of a dump truck.

As the instruments dozed on picnic benches
we warmed our gritty feet by the bonfire

and my new friend asked me if I was single.
You weren't there. I pondered my relationship

to verb tense, how I already miss
the present while it happens—those hands

of smoke carding my hair, tubas in dark water,
stars rushing to devour the hot forest sky,

inflamed and purpled all the way down
to the horizon line. And I am so far away

from where I started in this desert canyon
on the longest night of the longest year,

where the road seems to have been built
to adore you in your dips and swells

behind violet rock guardians who allow
you to slingshot and fall, recalling

that you are but one of them, as they are
but one of you—you who have followed

me all my life like the love who waits
for me to remember how I'd search

for you in the night skies of my infancy
before I even understood who you are,

for the moment when I'd find you
and your name flung from its orbit,

burst my synapses into satellites,
and I opened my mouth to speak.

The Sea Urchin Spines

—Island of Čiovo, Croatia

I don't think I'm doing a very good job.
          You've propped your heel on my knee

as I'm bowed over your big toe, trying
          and failing to dig out the black grit

with tweezers. You are not a reckless person,
          but the sea roils with creatures

that bite and sting. Even in turquoise,
          you can't always determine where to go.

I've started to consider that time passes
          differently for each of us. Weeks later

in research I discover that a vinegar soak
          dissolves calcium spikes. They move

slowly, these urchins, crawling with tube feet
          or pushing themselves gently

with points that reach and feel. What they eat
          must be even slower, or sessile.

Their version of mouths, mistranslated
          to *Aristotle's lantern*. Their whole bodies,

the old word for *hedgehog*. Don't we all live
          with the sea under our skin, unaware

of our own symmetry until we've hardened?
          Some hours, you stay fixed in place.

Some dawns, you wake and dive into the blue
          salt of grief where I cannot swim to you,

and I've started to consider acceptance,
          the way it slows everything down.

Their shells are called *tests* but only after
          they're gone. Eventually I must surrender

my warm water basin and boiled pinchers, too.
          You walk in pain like you always do

as I look on. In some versions urchin shells
          resemble thunderbolts, become magic

amulets that protect us from lightning
          and other harm. I know it's too much

to ask for no more harm. I cannot do anything
          to make things right. In every version I wait

on the shore for you to emerge.
          Empathy isn't what I thought it would be.

Ceres in the Permafrost Thaw

Stunned, how I looked back

I tried to redeem men

What structural failure

this is the state you wanted.

I can't deny I felt

Stone rings shifted

porous whorls. Almost

on my breath. Natural

save for the geometry

my protruding garden

postmodern opportunist

in moist-wintered forests,

Nowhere is safe from men

not coastlines, not history

can't escape a gold rush.

when you left me.

Where can I vanish

I have to believe I can

and saw myself living inside a pattern:

with other men. What borehole.

on my end. What ice lens. After everything,

This is your world.

cracks forming at the bog's edge.

the quilted ground in fine-grained,

beautiful if not for your palm

repository for ancient life, unmapped

of underground dens and burrows—

is not for sale. Except for you,

who unearths my secrets for profit

profit in continental shelves.

and their hands. Not riverbanks,

of the body in decay. Extinction

I was foolish to think you'd leave me

Where is my northerly island?

from the mathematics of shame?

rewrite this story from the ground up,

invent a new beginning

no one's heard before, neither spoken

aloud nor written down.

Can you see all of me more clearly

this time? My weapons—

oh, my mouth's full of them. What knives.

If I Misread a Word That Scares Me

—Ever: from Old English: feorhlīf ("life")

then each letter that follows has a memory
long as a shelf of ice. Each letter is a notch
in the doorframe of an old house even spirits
can't afford. Little piece of plastic, everlasting
as any container. I hate rules but I fear them.
Sometimes I get so defensive I start crying
and can't figure out why. What if each letter
is a striped piglet, a striped black and yellow
butterfly? Why is it I feel this need to describe
every damn thing that I see? If your hand
deceives you, it is your neck. If your neck
believes you, it is a river. I have been told
I paint in broad strokes. I have been labeled
volatile compound. I'm not sure if this is right,
but I think wanting to die from depression
is different than wanting to die out of fear.
Sometimes I miss depression. You don't care
whether you live or die, which is much easier
on the heart. Fear makes me have to track
my blood pressure, which creates more fear.
At all times; always. I'm not afraid of working
memory, but I think the reason I'm scared
of getting into trouble is because I don't
always want to be seen. I watched the video
of the sand dollar burying itself in minerals.
I watched the white bird flying into the night
storm clouds, assured as a moving star.
If there's this thing called *biophilia hypothesis*,
then there's a proposed explanation about love
of life or living systems, a basis of reasoning
without any assumption of its truth. *At any
time, in every way.* I guess I feel like if I don't
describe everything I see, then I won't exist
anymore. Because that's what actually happens.
There's proof. Ice is a living thing that dies.

The Doom

My pupils stung
I was told
pages where I imagined
they couldn't save me
the way they yelled
to live on
they reminded you of
how rain isn't just rain
existentially safe
on the window pane
where she lies pressed
a tender blot on the glass
at first I thought
but little did I know

blackened for hours
like a child
I was playing
on the day I might've died
it made me believe
you were climbing
Ireland in the sunshine
a whole season of it here
in your arms
forms an ethereal circle
against pea green mist
a figment I looked behind
the color wash of
that's how they like it

naturally wide-eyed
cradling her books and blank
with characters
they called me in the morning
no one in the world wanted me
above the river upon cliffs
we never talk about
I wish I could feel
the way condensation
around my sleeping cat
it stays when she leaves
my eyeball in the computer
blood would be my ending
nice and dark

All Your Gods Are Gaslighters

Where I live, birds take to the sky
like dragons—cranes and wood storks,

white-phase blue heron. In my mind
they are women. Powerful.

I have this power,
too, but I don't think it matters.

These women—I search for them
in stories: the goddess of vegetation,

the daughter of a nocturnal god,
beings from an archaic world

whose heads are cut and wrought
as weapons, tongues malformed

into swallows. Alone, I watch
the six-part documentary series

and stumble over the words
I've shoved beneath a wetland

of grease and fog... *He would build
me up then he would break me...*

then... then... Sometimes I think I see
a face staring at me from the roadkill.

Sometimes I think we were all used
by the same god. But nobody needs

another litany. *I started to believe
that I was nothing without... that he became...*

powerful. These women
ascend and I watch from below:

the one with her glinting silver
feathers—airborne, suspended in light,

she's a dagger, an arrow, a sword.

Princess Mononoke Hits Differently Now

The first time I watched it, I remember being floored
that Iron Town's ruler, Lady Eboshi—who I actually
kind of liked, even though I maybe wasn't supposed
to, because she wanted what she could name—
really shoots off the Forest Spirit's head. I didn't believe
she'd follow through with it once she sees him
with her own eyes. Now I'm like, *Seems about right.*
I suppose we all want to show everyone we know
how to kill a god of life and death. We can all be
short-sighted sometimes, and we'll do anything
to feel in control. I thought about the Night-Walker,
the Forest Spirit's nocturnal form, the other evening
when my boyfriend and I went a little wayward
on a nature trail after we lost track of time. The sky
was violaceous. The sky was amaranthine and studded
with bats flying more like moths than any bird until
it darkened suddenly as though from under a spilled glass
of wine. Neither of us cared. My legs ached pleasantly.
Sweat drizzled between my breasts. We were alone
in our own minds, in the memories we translate
to each other that'll always remain slightly mythological,
as in both a solace and a warning. The whole point
of stories. I thought about why the Forest Spirit changes.
When I was young I perceived him as the night sky
within a body that reflects and guards. He was the God
I believed in, watching over us, and I felt righteous
and secure. Now I wonder if he wasn't doing anything,
just walking around. During the day plants burst
fern-like from his steps. His body, a deer's with a great
furred chest. Instead of antlers, his head's a tree
with many branches. His face, a mask with direct eyes
and an omniscient smile. His blood cures wounds
but won't lift curses. Some acts even a god can't amend.
Lady Eboshi, I've been meaning to ask you for years
now: What did you think was going to happen?

How do you really kill a god? Dark on darkness
surrounding us almost makes us light. A rabbit sounds
larger than it is. Lavender wildflowers glow against
their eclipsed field. I believe a god is every generation.
Like people, his search destroys everything he touches
until they give him back his head. I thought about
how the forest grows again but is never going to be his.
Are we supposed to feel comforted? Are we supposed
to feel afraid? Maybe the whole point is to feel
neither, to surrender to the story's end. Movement
even within shadows. We watch deer leaping into night.

Ceres in the Cyber Apocalypse

At the end of the world there was always

going to be a woman

alone and digitally vulnerable,

shucked like drought corn, squalid as hair.

All I have ever asked for

was a pig and the other pig

inside her, born only in dreamtime.

You thought I wanted them slaughtered? How like a man

to see limitations for blood.

Believing you have power

will get you so far—you steal

my money by vowing you'll keep it safe,

cradle my passwords as if they were white-fuzz

caterpillars tumbling from your arms,

hold hostage photographs of my naked breasts

and the places where I'm hinged. Fine. Show it all,

take it all—what do you think I've kept

for myself? Spelt falls

from my open palms. I only have bread

and a daughter, bread and a daughter to give you.

Don't you know I can't leave

her even if I'm halved and scooped

of seeds faint as insect wings? I emerged from the earth

like a plant and I will depart

like a plant if you force me to:

bloodless, voiceless, how my body weighs

heavy as a riverbed in the dry loam. My final

exhale rises. I become the air you breathe.

Before the Formal Feeling – Darkness

*"After starting this Rx, you may experience suicidal ideation.
These thoughts should pass in time."*

—Lines adapted from Emily Dickinson

Before I chose this single star – Worlds scoop their Arcs inside me. Before Powder exists in Charcoal – I feel so old a pain. Before This, and my heart, and all the fields – A few prosaic days. Before My syllable rebelled – In horrid, hooting stanza. Before The House was hooked and wanting – A ribbon at a time. Before My Mind was going numb – It made an Even Face. Before the frock I wept in – Caress my freezing hair. Before in sleep – All Hue forgotten – I dance like a bomb. Before I'm done with chart and compass – My river waits reply. Before my soft inhabitants – I'm bursting all the doors. Before where Oceans are – and Prayer –that's Where the Meanings lie. Before the light – and me besides – I would not admit the wound. Before I saw my Brain – go round – I dared in lonely Place. Before I fought aloud and louder – I felt the power to die. Before This World was not Conclusion – my low feet staggered home. Before I remembered to speak again – I could not breathe without a key.

Love When It's Hard

For years I predicted the behavior of my heart:
heavy with protein, a sea-worn block of wood,
it'd fill any interior with rubble, the innermost part

of a city whose lamplit corners I learned by rote.
A student of logic, I devised a formula that could
test conditions of the soil, but the heart

doesn't belong on steady ground. It's a spark
from a match I felt too hesitant to strike in good
conscience. So I analyzed but never knew my heart.

When I resolved to stop breaking, I studied the art
of hiding within syntax, masking my eyes with soot.
A dense cluster of leaves forms a cabbage heart

and I burrowed myself down there. In the dark
I could be bracketed or abbreviated, misunderstood
as a secret. Even then, the musculature of my heart

regenerated, a faithful paper crane. I never thought
it would be you—not by chance but by one foot
trailing the other in wet grass. Our hearts
decided to carry on together, ready to do the work.

Walking with You in the Town Where I Used to Live

Here is where the path flooded. Here is where I turned

        back and found a new way to go. Where the redwing

blackbird clawed at my scalp. Where the hawk circled

        the carved stones. Here is where I saw the dying

coyote, and here is where the petticoats of bluebells still grow.

        Little crosses in the dogwood. Little mushrooms

seasoning the biscuits and gravy. You eat every salted crumb

        I leave behind, and I teach you the frenzied flush

of crabapple, the tulip poplar's mittened hands.

        This is the time of year when I choose to return:

a dull, scabbed-over beauty in Midwestern spring,

        trusted friend with hazel eyes. I barely knew

you when I lived here. We talked once about "The River."

        I played a prisoner in your scene. When we met—

sweltering room, a purple dress, it was so long ago.

        Here is where bats shiver the darkening redbuds.

Here is where the woodpecker flutes his bug-hunting song.

        I say *wood* instead of *bud*. Instead of *red*, you say

rose. Here are the winter pies baked in a strip mall.

        Here is my sunburnt neck, your sunburnt nose.

Here are the free libraries painted like birdhouses

        where anyone can open the chambers, take a book

from their hearts. Here is where we reach for each other

        in the path and in the road—here and here

and here again. No one tells you when a river runs dry

       or when it will overflow. No one tells you

who will be there when it does. At night, we walk back

       to your apartment. Here is where our Pink Moon

rises beyond the exit ramp, not unlike the morning

       sun. Yellow as a campfire, big as a home.

I thought it was a sign. It wasn't. We don't need one.

Succulent in Chains

I am more than a piece of living art. I continue and endure.
Who else thrives on neglect? Forsake my Latin name. I endure

the agony of your garden, your Scripture-based words. Rosary
vine, some call me, or string of hearts, gray-patterned to endure

your insufficient sun. String of pearls, string of nickels, string
of buttons, string of beads. I depreciate in value, endure

your laconic metaphors. My flowers bloom in little water, white
and cinnamon-scented. To group in clusters is a way to endure

loneliness, but I am more than a conversation piece. Lamb's tail,
string of turtles, string of fishhooks, string of dolphins—I endure

the curse of becoming more similar as I grow. You can't tell me
apart from me, my petals insignificant and cream. They'll endure

your worth based on numbers. I am a string of tears, forever
storing water. I gather without yielding: it's how I will survive.

Ceres in the Environmental Personhood

Listen, I don't want to leave my job. I just want an apology
because it's not my fault that you were made stupid
by the fear of blasphemy, which is really your own need
for control over other minds. A person cannot be owned
so therefore, neither can a river. Neither forest nor field.
All living systems share a common destiny—indivisible
and whole from the mountains to the sea, the right to exist,
to persist, to maintain and regenerate their vital cycles.
A goddess belongs to herself, which is to say I don't belong
to your environment or your economy if I choose
my shipwrecked existence, my dark-walled home.
Here is the world's greatest secret: my daughter lives
in art and summer and golden leaves. I have no daughter
or I have every one. She is the personification of vegetation.
I am the mother of the goddess of death: savior maiden,
bringer of fruit, child of bread. Here is the greater secret
no one wants you to know: she went willingly in search
of her own depth and power. That means I must go, too.

The Solar Eclipse Sends Me into a Panic at Eight Years Old and Again at Thirty-One

Still, I am trying to understand why
        I've ignored those oysters of light

                that wink among tree shadows
      until they tremble in a strange tide.

The moon draws salt crescents on the sidewalk
        as though a child, and I'm well aware

                that I can bum out everyone
      around me with my initial read

of any crowd. I'm not here for good
        vibes, though I've learned to keep

                this to myself most of the time.
      Sensitivity to lunar nodes is not a great way

to make friends, and I'm the one whose glands
        ache from a hangnail or sty. But flowers close.

                Spiders begin to undress their orbs,
      hippos return to their night islands

and bees fly back to their hives (cows don't
        give a shit, true earth signs) and lemurs freeze

                in their perches, so then why shouldn't I?
      Even Christ was born from a star and died

in celestial darkness—torn cloth, torn sky.
        Why do I hear clocks ticking all at once

while everyone else seems fine?
I am trying to understand the difference

between fear in the body and fear in the mind.
And it's hard to admit sometimes that I'm still

eight and nine and ten inside.
But maybe my younger selves always lie

shingled in wait for me to gaze up and find
that delicate smile brimmed with blood.

This is the real wonder of it all:
a primeval fear locked in my mind

unloosened by patterns, logic, or rhyme
that thrills me from my hiding place

out into a world of change.
How ancient my brain! How animal and alive!

The Rainy Season

raises up animals from their water houses:
     birds like wet laundry, alligators close enough to appear
long-lashed and serene, Florida chicken turtle

     bundled in the apartment parking lot
as though delivered by drone. It's a choking hazard
     down here, May to October, a mouthful

of black grapes, head rush of supernatural and melodrama,
     and when the crepe myrtle's bubblegum wig
starts to shake, I can't foretell

     what may or may not descend. What ruin
or what cleanse. Lightning skewers a sun halo,
     toothpick in hors d'oeuvres. And just today I saw

the place where a rainbow ends. It's mostly green,
     graphic arc and intersection, fleeting
as a page in the Book of Common Prayer I mark and enter

     when the apocalypse in my brain arrests me
that in light we may see light and I feel a desire to be lifted,
     too. I want my heart to be drawn

and my imagination filled with what comes
     after mercy—storm, flood, an ending not
in archway but in smokescreen

     where sunset amends the rain
clouds like you've never seen a fire without flames.
     That's when the sweetest blue

yawns in soft pearls—color that can only be painted,
     that belongs deep inside a seashell
or a body in love, tenderness I almost can't believe I deserve.

Serenade with Siren and Coyotes

—for V. H.

You said if nothing is a home then everything
        can be, so for tonight we are home together,

newly together, entwined on an air mattress
        in my childhood friend's guest room.

Come dawn, we will fly back to our cities,
        half a country apart. One hour apart:

the difference between daybreak
        and morning, dusk and nightfall.

Maybe the clocks really did stop
        two years ago. Maybe we both

had to surrender to arrive. How did I find you,
        amidst miasma and pall?

Born half a planet from each other.
        Born in less than a month of winter sun.

When we were children, we both lost our homes.
        When we were children, we lived

through the deadliest tornado
        in the county, the war that stole

fathers, siege of bombs that wouldn't end.
        Does anything ever end? Pain, fear—

if one begins to fade, the other
        cleaves tighter. This is the way of it:

open window above us, sheets cool
        and green as ferns, we slip into the hour

between breath and skin. *Listen.*
           We still. How many streets away,

an ambulance trills out the worst moments
           of someone else's life.

It's then we hear them harmonize—the coyotes
           we couldn't know would arise

in the hour we are all made animals,
           in the sound that lifts up

the streets, the trees, the houses suspended
           like the shape of mist that has yet

to dissolve. There isn't much I can research.
           There isn't much I can say.

We speak a song, and it plays.
           I am not afraid to call its name.

Here we are. Here we are. We hold
           each other close and listen to the howls.

My Poems Keep Ending in Stars

Which means I can't stop thinking
about the dying

passage of time. Which means I experience
flashing sensations, as from a blow

to the head. Sudden white spot
on the forehead

of a horse. An ancient
and forgotten name. Uncreated

god. Which means I fall enraptured,
as with romantic love.

To set with small, bright bodies.
To buy an additional life

or lives. Which means I burn
high in the air with a colored flame.

Which means I crack
into radiating contours. I release

my units of power. Naked body
under a vast night sky. Crown of thorns

in the seas of hard coral. I pour out
only the water that is required.

Which means I am affixed
with my own distinctive purpose.

Which means I learned to gem
and sequin. Vulnerable

as a necklace. Subconscious
and granular. Which means I count

feathers and jasmine. Leather
and pink sand. Which means I test

my faith even as I kneel on dry land.
Which means that I begin.

Notes

A note on the title: I first came across the word "everywhen" while reading David Wallace-Wells' article "The Uninhabitable Earth," originally published in *New York Magazine* on July 10, 2017. He explains that the term is synonymous with "dreamtime," an idea coined by Aboriginal Australians, to depict a real-world-mythical realm of gods and mortals, the past and present happening all at once. Wallace-Wells likens "everywhen" or "dreamtime" to the Anthropocene, this era when history catches up to our current moment and we feel the consequences of long-ago decisions suddenly upon us. This collapse of linear chronology, this awareness of time being out of joint, terrified and thrilled me. What's more, I initially misread the term "everywhen" as "everwhen," the inverse of "whenever." After years passed and I finally realized my mistake, I wondered if my brain had misread this word on purpose, working all the while to invent my own sense of time-out-of-time.

The epigraphs at the beginning of the book are from *The Mushroom at the End of the World: On the Possibility of Life in Capitalist Ruins* by Anna Lowenhaupt Tsing (Princeton University Press) and *The Odyssey* by Homer, translated by Emily Wilson (W.W. Norton & Company, Inc.).

"I Begin in Scrolls" loosely incorporates traditional story-starting and story-ending phrases from languages around the world, including Algerian Arabic, Amharic, Armenian, Catalan, Czech, Esperanto, German, Gujarati, Moroccan Arabic, Persian, Polish, Slovak, and Spanish.

The Ceres poems are written in the voice of the Roman goddess of agriculture, women and girls, and cereal grains, as imagined in the twentieth century Anthropocene. Ceres is the Roman counterpart of the Greek goddess Demeter, the mother of Persephone.

The italicized words *backed and packed* in "A Lot of Stuff Happened and I Quit Being Normal" are from the Elizabeth Bishop poem "The Fish."

"The Lamp Inside" also references the Elizabeth Bishop poem "In the Waiting Room."

"I Tell My Sister I Learned Space is Like a Donut" is in memory of Monica A. Hand.

"The Hibiscus Talked to Me" takes its title from the last line of Chavali Bangaramma's poem "Hibiscus on the Lake."

"Heather Lives in Missouri and I Live in Florida but our Friend is Very Sick in California and We Want to Light a Candle" and "I Proofread My Friend's Last Essay" are in memory of Naira Kuzmich.

"Serenade with Siren and Coyotes" is for Vedran Husić.

Acknowledgments

Many thanks to the editors of the journals where these poems first appeared, some in slightly different versions:

The Account: "Ceres in the Red Tide" and "Ceres in the Global Heatwave"

Arts & Letters: "The Sea Urchin Spines" and "Love When It's Hard"

Atticus Review: "Ceres in the Cyber Apocalypse"

Aquifer: The Florida Review Online: "The Night My Number Tripled"

Bear Review: "Künstlerroman" and "The Lamp Inside"

Blood Orange Review: "Ceres in the Permafrost Thaw"

Boulevard: "To the Solstice Moon over Red Rock Canyon"

CAROUSEL Magazine: "The Hibiscus Talked to Me"

Cold Mountain Review: "Ceres in the Mass Extinction"

Colorado Review: "Aubade with Myself Leaving Myself Behind" and "The Cats of Imerovigli"

Couplet Poetry: "Ceres in the Field of Bones" and "Ceres in the Environmental Personhood"

deComp: "The Crying Bird"

Diode Poetry Journal: "All Your Gods Are Gaslighters"

Four Way Review: "Elegy for Fallen Palms" and "I Always Wanted to Save the Rainforest"

Ecotone: "Ceres in the Burning Rainforest"

Hobart: "Ceres in the Uncreation"

The Los Angeles Review: "So This is What It Means to Be Alone" and "My Poems Keep Ending in Stars"

NELLE: "Persona Poem"

New Orleans Review: "The Rainy Season"

The Normal School: "The Prayer Plant Speaks" and "Walking with You in the Town Where I Used to Live"

Pinwheel: "Pelvic Ultrasound"

The Poetry Review: "A Lot of Stuff Happened, and I Quit Being Normal"

Saw Palm: florida literature and art: "Heather Lives in Missouri and I Live in Florida but our Friend is Very Sick in California and We Want to Light a Candle"

South Dakota Review: "My Hair Falls Out"

Southern Humanities Review: "Owls Come to Us"

The Spectacle: "Tennessee is Burning," "Why I Couldn't Write," "I Tell My Sister I Learned Space Is Like a Donut" (originally titled "Final Days, 2016")

Superstition Review: "The Solar Eclipse Sends Me into a Panic at Eight Years Old and Again at Thirty-One"

SWWIM Every Day: "I Serve My God a Pineapple Upside-Down Cake"

Waxwing Literary Journal: "I Begin in Scrolls" and "I Proofread My Friend's Last Essay"

Willow Springs: "*Princess Mononoke* Hits Differently Now"

The Worcester Review: "If I Misread a Word That Scares Me"

"A Lot of Stuff Happened, and I Quit Being Normal" was translated into Turkish by İrem Kargıoğlu.

The original version of "I Tell My Sister I Learned Space is Like a Donut" (originally titled "Final Days, 2016") was translated into Russian by Tatyana Melochikhina.

"Pelvic Ultrasound" was selected and featured by Tracy K. Smith on the podcast *The Slowdown*.

"Aubade with Myself Leaving Myself Behind" was selected and reprinted by J. P. Dancing Bear in *Verse Daily*.

∞

Thank you to Mary Biddinger, Amy Freels, Jon Miller, and everyone at The University of Akron Press. You bring my books home.

Thank you to my students and colleagues at Saint Leo University, and especially to Kathryn Duncan and Allyson Marino.

Thank you to my Reynolds community—fire and friendship, always.

Thank you to Avni Vyas for all the Florida adventures, the poetry, and for always being there for me (even in the middle of a Janelle Monáe concert).

Thank you to Heather McGuire and J. D. Smith. You are my family.

Thank you to Brandi Nicole Martin, my loyal friend and the first editor for everything I write.

Thank you to Nancy and Scott Barngrover; Kristy, James, Cassidy, and Logan Clear; my grandparents; and to Ben Barngrover, who turned many of these poems into songs.

And thank you, thank you, to Vedran Husić—my best reader, my lodestar. I love you.

Photo: Heather McGuire

Anne Barngrover is most recently the author of *Brazen Creature* (University of Akron Press, 2018). Her poems and creative nonfiction have appeared in such places as *Verse Daily*, *Arts & Letters*, *Guernica*, *Ecotone*, and *The Slowdown* podcast. She directs the low-residency MA in Creative Writing program at Saint Leo University and lives in Tampa, Florida.